COVERING ALL THE VOCABULARY OF

'READING GREEK'
SECTIONS 1 - 9
- FLASHCARDS TO GO -

Flashcards are a great way to study!
If you are about to learn new vocabulary, flashcards can make the job so much easier. Flashcards are effective because they are founded on the principles of rote learning and memorization.

These flashcards are two-sided study aids that have ancient Greek words on one side, and the English translation on the opposite side. You are able to increase the difficulty by putting easy ones aside and focusing on the more difficult.

Using flashcards is a very effective strategy for studying - at home or on the go.
The flashcards travel with you and are useful for a quick review and a convenient study tool at bus stops, waiting in a line or on any occasion you have some free time.

Continuously reviewing your flashcards will ensure that you'll retain more of the information that you're studying with little effort required.

JUST CUT,
FOLD,
GLUE,
FIND A BOX

AND START ENJOYING WITHOUT WORRIES

THE BEAUTY OF ANCIENT GREEK ....

My best experienced-based tools for easy learning :

1.Tool for easy learning :

!!!!!!! For better memorization - especially in the beginning of your study- write on each flashcard how you would write this word with your own letters or how you would pronounce it in your own language.

example :

το νεωριον (- I used for myself following way :) * tŏ neōriŏn * (ō = long o, ŏ = short o)	dockyard

Note :

Every word beginning with a vowel (α, ε, η, ι, ο, υ, ω) or rho (ρ) has a tiny mark above it. That mark is known as a 'breathing'. In Ancient Greek you find 2 types of breathings :

A 'rough' breathing written above a vowel (looks a bit like half of a circle open to the right) indicates that the word is pronounced with an initial 'h' sound.
Thus the word for a 'boundary stone' is : **ὁ**ρος (pronounced : **h**oros).

A 'smooth' breathing written above a vowel (looks like half of a circle open to the left) indicates the absence of an 'h' sound. Thus the word for mountain is : ὀρος (pronounced : oros).

2. Tool for easy learning :

!!!!!! To make things more easy to study I omitted all the smooth breathings at the beginning of the words (just remember to write them in your assignments / exams !!!).

3. Tool for easy learning :

!!!!! Learn from the start the words plus the initial 'h' sound. Example : ὁρος (horos).
I highlighted in grey all the words beginning with rough breathings.

(Always include breathings when writing. Omitting them means a spelling mistake !!!)

4. Tool for easy learning :

!!!!! Learn from the start the noun plus the article. Example : **ὁ** **ὁ**ρος (ho horos)

Note :

For easy memorization I split up the verbs into the stem plus the first person singular ending: διωκ - **ω** = **I** chase οβε - **ομαι** = **I** fear

For better memorization I split up the words into pieces that you already would know:
example: αποβαινω **:** απο - βαιν **- ω :** (meaning : I leave, depart)
απο = away βαιν = go ω = I

For easy memorization I split up the adjectives into the stem plus masc./fem./neutr. forms.
Example: θνητ **- ος** the mortal (man e.g.)
- η the mortal (woman e.g)
- ον ......

For easy memorization I split up the adverbs into the stem and the ending **- ως** in order to indicate that the word is an adverb.
Example : σαφ **- ως** (meaning : 'clearly')

Best tool for easy learning :

The best ways to learn ancient Greek is to adopt a study pattern of **'little and often'.**

Vocabulary 1 A - B :

20 cards

'Reading Greek'

ἡ ακροπολις

Acropolis

1 A-B

αρα

(indicates a question)

1 A-B

βαιν - **ω**

I come,
I go,
I walk

1 A-B

ἡ γη

land

1 A-B

δε

and,
bu

1 A-B

δευρο

over here

1 A-B

εγω

I

1 A-B

επειτα

then,
next

1 A-B

Greek	Ref.	English
και	1 A-B	and, also
καλ - **ος** **- η** **- ον**	1 A-B	beautiful, fine, good
ὁ ναυτης	1 A-B	sailor
το νεωριον	1 A-B	dockyard
ὁ **ἡ** **το**	1 A-B	the
ὁ Παρθενων	1 A-B	the Parthenon
το πλοιον	1 A-B	vessel, ship
ὁ ῥαψωδος	1 A-B	rhapsode
συ	1 A-B	you (singular)

Greek	Lesson	English
τε....και	1 A-B	A and B, both A and B, both....and....
τίς	1 A-B	who ? what ?
ω	1 A-B	O .... (addressing someone)

Vocabulary 1 C- D :

19 words

'Reading Greek'

ακου - **ω**		**I** hear, **I** listen
	1 C-D	
(**τα**) αληθη		the truth
	1 C-D	
αλλα		but, alternatively
	1 C-D	
βλεπ - **ω**		**I** look (at)
	1 C-D	
γαρ		for, because
	1 C-D	
διωκ - **ω**		**I** chase, **I** pursue **I** prosecute
	1 C-D	
εγωγε		I at least, I at any rate
	1 C-D	
εισ - βαιν - **ω**		**I** enter, **I** board
	1 C-D	
ἡμεις		we
	1 C-D	

Greek	Ref.	English
κατα-βαιν - **ω**	1 C-D	**I** go down, **I** come down
μεν - **ω**	1 C-D	**I** remain, **I** wait for
μη	1 C-D	don't ! not
ου, ουκ, ουχ	1 C-D	no, not
ουδεν	1 C-D	nothing
ουν	1 C-D	so, then, really, therefore
τί ;	1 C-D	what ?
ὑμεις	1 C-D	you (plural)
φευγ - **ω**	1 C-D	**I** flee, **I** run away, **I** run off, **I** am a defendant, **I** am on trial

ὠς

how !

1 C-D

Vocabulary 1 E-F

14 words

'Reading Greek'

ακριβ - **ως**	1 E-F	accurately, closely
βαθε - **ως**	1 E-F	deeply
βοηθε - **ω**	1 E-F	**I** help, **I** run to help
δηλο - **ω**	1 E-F	**I** show, **I** reveal
κακ - **ως**	1 E-F	badly, evilly
καλ - **ως**	1 E-F	finely, beautifully
μεν…δε	1 E-F	on the one hand……on the other
οιμοι	1 E-F	alas ! oh dear !
ὁρα - **ω**	1 E-F	**I** see

ποι ;	1 E-F	to where ?
ποιε - **ω**	1 E-F	**I** make, **I** do
που ;	1 E-F	where (at) ?
σαφ - **ως**	1 E-F	clearly
σεαυτ - ον - ην	1 E-F	yourself (singular)

Vocabulary 1 G

31 words

'Reading Greek'

ανα - βαιν - **ω**		1 G	**I** go up
ὁ ανθρωπος		1 G	man, fellow
απο	(+ genitive)	1 G	away from
απο - θνησκ - **ω**		1 G	**I** die
απο - χωρε - **ω**		1 G	**I** go away, **I** depart
γε		1 G	at least, at any rate
δια τι ;		1 G	why **?**
δυ - **ω**		1 G	**I** sink
εις	(+ acc.)	1 G	to, into, onto

εκ , εξ (+ gen.)	1 G	out of
ελθε	1 G	come ! go !
το εμποριον	1 G	market-hall, trading-post
εν (+ dat.)	1 G	in
το εργον	1 G	task, work, job, duty
εχ - **ω**	1 G	**I** have, **I** hold
ἡμετερ - **ος** - **α** - **ον**	1 G	our(s)
ἡ θαλαττα	1 G	sea
kak - **ως** - **η** - **ον**	1 G	bad,evil, cowardly, lowly, mean

ὁ κυβερνητης 1 G		captain, helmsman
λεγ - **ω** 1 G		**I** say
ὁ λεμβος 1 G		boat, life-boat
νυν 1 G		now
πλε - **ω** 1 G		**I** sail
προς 1 G	(+ acc.)	towards
ῥ ι π τ - **ω** 1 G		I throw, I hurl
σωζ - **ω** 1 G		**I** save, **I** keep safe
σω **- ος** **- α** **- ον** 1 G		safe

ἡ σωτηρια	1 G	safety, salvation
ὁ φιλος	1 G	friend
φιλ - **ος** - **η** - **ον**	1 G	dear, friendly, one's own
φροντιζ - **ω**	1 G	I think, I worry

Vocabulary 1 H-J

21 words

'Reading Greek'

αει	1 H-J	always
αριστ - **ος** - **η** - **ον**	1 H-J	best, very good
γιγνωσκ - **ω**	1 H-J	**I** know **I** think **I** resolve
δηλ - **ος** - **η** - **ον**	1 H-J	clear, obvious
ειμι	1 H-J	I am
ὁ Ἑλλην	1 H-J	Greek
εμπειρ - **ος** - **ον**	1 H-J	skilled experienced
η	1 H-J	or

μωρ - **ος** - **α** - **ον**	1 H-J	stupid, foolish
ναι	1 H-J	yes
ἡ ναυς	1 H-J	ship
οιδα	1 H-J	I know
ὁτι	1 H-J	that (**ὁ...**)
παιζ - **ω**	1 H-J	**I** play, **I** joke (at)
περι (+ acc.)	1 H-J	about
πολλα	1 H-J	many things
πως γαρ ου	1 H-J	of course

ὁ στρατηγος 1 H-J	general
τα ναυτικα 1 H-J	naval matters
τα στρατηγικα 1 H-J	leadership generalship
τα στρατιωτικα 1 H-J	military matters

Vocabulary 2 A-D

55 words

'Reading Greek'

αγαθ- **ος** - **η** - **ον**	2 A-D	good, noble, couragous
ὁ Αθηναιος	2 A-D	Athenian
ἁμα	2 A-D	at the same time
αναχωρε- **ω**	2 A-D	**I** retreat
απορε- **ω**	2 A-D	**I** am at a loss, **I** have no resources
ἡ απορια	2 A-D	perplexity, lack of provisions
αυθις	2 A-D	again
ὁ βαρβαρος	2 A-D	barbarian, foreigner

βεβαι- **ος** - **α** - **ον**		2 A-D	secure
βραδεως		2 A-D	slowly
δια	(+ acc)	2 A-D	because of
διερχ - **ομαι**		2 A-D	I go through, I relate
δουλο - **ομαι**		2 A-D	I enslave, I make X a slave
ἡ ελευθερια		2 A-D	freedom
ελευθερ - **ος** - **α** - **ον**		2 A-D	free
ελευθερο - **ω**		2 A-D	I free, I set free
εμ - **ος** - **η** - **ον**		2 A-D	my, mine

επειδη	2 A-D	when (ε...)
επερχ - **ομαι**	2 A-D	**I** go against, **I** attack
επι (+acc.)	2 A-D	at, against
ερχ - **ομαι**	2 A-D	**I** go, **I** come
ἡδεως	2 A-D	with pleasure, happily
ηδη	2 A-D	by now, now, already
ἡσυχαζ - **ω**	2 A-D	**I** am quiet, **I** keep quiet
ἡ ἡσυχια	2 A-D	quiet, peace
ἡ θεα	2 A-D	goddess

Greek	Ref.	English
θεα - **ομαι**	2 A-D	I observe, I watch, I gaze at
καλλιστ - **ος** - **η** - **ον**	2 A-D	very fine, very beautiful, very good, finest, most beautiful, best
ὁ λογος	2 A-D	word, speech, story, tale, reason, argument
μαχ - **ομαι**	2 A-D	I fight
ἡ ναυμαχια	2 A-D	naval battle, sea- battle
νικα - **ω**	2 A-D	I win, I defeat
ἡ νικη	2 A-D	victory, conquest
ἡ **ὁ**μονοια	2 A-D	agreement, harmony
ὁσ - **ος** - **η** - **ον**	2 A-D	how great ! as much as, as many as

Greek	Ref.	English
ουκετι	2 A-D	no longer
οὑτω(ς)	2 A-D	thus, so, in this way
παρα (+ acc.)	2 A-D	along, alongside , against
π ι π τ - **ω**	2 A-D	**I** fall, **I** die
οι πολεμιοι	2 A-D	enemy
πολεμι - **ος** / - **α** / - **ον**	2 A-D	hostile, enemy
ὁ πολεμος	2 A-D	war
ποτερον…η	2 A-D	whether....or
προσερχ - **ομαι**	2 A-D	**I** advance, **I** go towards, **I** come towards

σιωπα - **ω** 2 A-D	**I** am silent
σκοπε - **ω** 2 A-D	**I** look (at), **I** consider
ἡ στρατια 2 A-D	army
ταχεως 2 A-D	quickly
τελος 2 A-D	in the end, finally
τι 2 A-D	a, something
ἡ τολμα 2 A-D	daring
τολμα - **ω** 2 A-D	**I** dare, **I** am daring, **I** undertake
φοβε - **ομαι** 2 A-D	**I** fear, **I** am afraid (of)

ψευδ - **ως**

falsely

2 A-D

ὡσπερ

like,
as

2 A-D

Vocabulary 3 A - E

63 words

'Reading Greek'

αγε	3 A-E	come !
αλληλους	3 A-E	each other, one another
αλλ - **ος** **- η** **- ο**	3 A-E	other, the rest of
ὁ ανηρ	3 A-E	man
αφικνε - **ομαι**	3 A-E	I arrive, I come
βοα - **ω**	3 A-E	I shout (for)
ὁ γειτων	3 A-E	neighbour
δειν - **ος** **- η** **- ον**	3 A-E	terrible, dire, clever

δη	3 A-E	then, indeed
εγγυς	3 A-E	near, nearby
ειπε	3 A-E	speak ! tell me !
εκειν - **ος** / - **η** / - **ο**	3 A-E	that (ε...)
εμ - βαιν - **ω**	3 A-E	**I** embark
επειδη	3 A-E	when, since, because
ερωτα - **ω**	3 A-E	I ask
ετι	3 A-E	still, yet
ευ	3 A-E	well

ἡ ευχη 3 A-E	prayer
ευχ - **ομαι** 3 A-E	**I** pray
ὁ Ζευς 3 A-E	Zeus
ζητε - **ω** 3 A-E	**I** look for, **I** seek
ὁ θορυβος 3 A-E	noise, din, hustle and bustle
ἡ θυρα 3 A-E	door
ἡ θυσια 3 A-E	sacrifice
θυ - **ω** 3 A-E	**I** sacrifice
ιδου 3 A-E	look ! here ! hey !

καθευδ - **ω**	3 A-E	I sleep
καλε - **ω**	3 A-E	I call, I summon
κατα	3 A-E	in, on, by, according to
ὁ κελευστης	3 A-E	boatswain
κελευ - **ω**	3 A-E	I order
ὁ κινδυνος	3 A-E	danger
ὁ Λακεδαιμονιος	3 A-E	Spartan
λαμβαν - **ω**	3 A-E	I take, I capture
ἡ λαμπας	3 A-E	torch, lamp

Greek	Ref.	English
ὁ λιμην	3 A-E	harbour
μανθαν - **ω**	3 A-E	I learn, I understand
μεγ - **ας** - **αλη** - **α**	3 A-E	big, great
ναυτικ - **ος** - **η** - **ον**	3 A-E	naval
ἡ νησος	3 A-E	island
ἡ νυξ	3 A-E	night
ἡ οικια	3 A-E	house
οικαδε	3 A-E	homewards
οικοι	3 A-E	at home

τα ὁπλα	3 A-E	weapons, arms
ουδε	3 A-E	and not, not even
οὑτος αὑτη !!! τουτο !!!	3 A-E	this
οὑτοσι αὑτηι !!! τουτι !!!	3 A-E	this here
ὁ παις	3 A-E	child, son, boy, slave
ἡ πατρις	3 A-E	fatherland
ποθεν **;**	3 A-E	from where **?**
πολυς πολλη !!! πολυ !!!	3 A-E	many, much
πορευ - **ομαι**	3 A-E	**I** march, **I** journey, **I** go

Greek	Ref.	English
τα πυρα	3 A-E	fire-signal
σπενδ - **ω**	3 A-E	**I** pour a libation
σπευδ - **ω**	3 A-E	**I** hurry
ἡ σπονδη	3 A-E	libation
ὁ σωτηρ	3 A-E	saviour
ἡ τεχνη	3 A-E	skill, art, expertise
τρεχ - **ω**	3 A-E	I run
ὁ τριηραρχος	3 A-E	trierarch
φαιν - **ομαι**	3 A-E	**I** appear, **I** seem, **I** seem to be

χωρε - **ω**

I go,
I come

3 A-E

Vocabulary 4 A-B

34 words

'Reading Greek'

το αστυ	4 A-E	city (of Athens)
ατιμαζ - **ω**	4 A-E	I dishonour, I hold in dishonour
ὁ γεωργος	4 A-E	farmer
ἡ γυνη	4 A-E	woman, wife
ὁ δαιμων	4 A-E	god, (minor) deity, daimon
ὁ δεσποτης	4 A-E	master
διαφθειρ - **ω**	4 A-E	I destroy, I kill, I corrupt
ετι και νυν	4 A-E	even now, still now

ευφρων	4 A-E	well- disposed
ὁ θεος **ἡ** θεος	4 A-E	god (-dess)
θνητ **- ος** **- η** **- ον**	4 A-E	mortal
κακο - δαιμ - **ων** - δαιμ - **ον**	4 A-E	unlucky, dogged by an evil daimon
κρατε **- ω**	4 A-E	**I** hold sway, **I** hold power (over)
κωλυ **- ω**	4 A-E	**I** prevent, **I** stop
μαλιστα	4 A-E	especially, particularly, yes
ὁ νεκρος	4 A-E	corpse
νη	4 A-E	by ….! (ν….)

ὁ νομος	4 A-E	law, convention
ἡ νοσος	4 A-E	plague, disease
ἡ οικησις	4 A-E	dwelling
ολιγ - **ος** - **η** - **ον**	4 A-E	small, few
ουδε - **ις** - **μια** - **ν**	4 A-E	no, no one, nothing
το πληθος	4 A-E	number, crowd, the people
ἡ πολις	4 A-E	city (state)
το πραγμα	4 A-E	thing, matter, affair troubles (plural)
ἡ πυρα	4 A-E	funeral pyre

Greek	Ref.	English
τα σκευη	4 A-E	gear, furniture
ἡ ταξις	4 A-E	battle- array, order, rank
τιμα - **ω**	4 A-E	I honour, I value, I reckon
τ**ί**ς τ**ί**	4 A-E	who ? what ?
τις τι	4 A-E	a, a certain, someone
τυπ τ - **ω**	4 A-E	I strike, I hit
φερ - **ω**	4 A-E	I carry, I bear, I endure, I lead
ὁ φοβος	4 A-E	fear

Vocabulary 4 C- D

30 words

'Reading Greek'

ἡ ανομια	4 C-D	lawlessness
απαγ - **ω**	4 C-D	**I** lead away **I** take away
απο - κτειν - **ω**	4 C-D	**I** kill
απο - φευγ - **ω**	4 C-D	**I** escape, **I** run off
ἡ ασεβεια	4 C-D	irreverence to the gods, impiety
αυτ - **ον** - **ην** - **ο**	4 C- D	him, her, it, them
αφελκ - **ω**	4 C-D	**I** drag off, I drag away
ὁ βασιλευς	4 C-D	king

Greek	Ref.	English
ὁ βωμος	4 C-D	altar
ὁ δουλος	4 C-D	slave
επι - καλε - **ομαι**	4 C-D	I call upon (to witness)
το ἱερον	4 C-D	sanctuary, temple
ὁ ἱκετης	4 C-D	suppliant
ὁ κηρυξ	4 C-D	herald
λανθαν **- ω**	4 C-D	I escape the notice of X in ….ing
μα	4 C-D	by …..! (μ…)
μισε **- ω**	4 C-D	I hate

Greek	Ref.	English
ὁ ξενος / ξεινος	4 C-D	foreigner, guest, host
ολοφυρ - **ομαι**	4 C-D	I lament, I mourn for
ορθ - **ος** - **η** - **ον**	4 C-D	straight, correct, right
π ασ χ - **ω**	4 C-D	I suffer, I experience, I undergo
παυ - **ομαι**	4 C-D	I cease
ὁ πρεσβευτης	4 C-D	ambassador
οι πρεσβεις	4 C-D	ambassadors
τρεπ - **ομαι**	4 C-D	I turn, I turn in flight
τυγχαν - **ω**	4 C-D	I happen to be ….ing, I am actually ….ing

ἡ **ὑ**βρις 4 C-D	aggression, violence
ὁ **ὑ**π ηρετης 4 C-D	servant, slave
φθαν **- ω** 4 C-D	**I** anticipate X in ….ing
ω 4 C-D	what …..! (exclamation)

Vocabulary 5 A-B :

33 words

'Reading Greek'

αιτι - **ος** **- α** **- ον**	5 A-B	responsible (for), guilty (of)
ἁ π τ - **ω**	5 A-B	**I** light, **I** fasten, **I** fix
βαθυς	5 A-B	deep
βαρυς	5 A-B	heavy
ὁ βιος	5 A-B	life, means, livelihood
ὁ γαμος	5 A-B	marriage
διαλεγ - **ομαι**	5 A-B	**I** converse
ἡ δικη	5 A-B	lawsuit, penalty, justice

δικην λαμβαν - **ω**	**I** exact my due, **I** punish	5 A-B
διοτι	because	5 A-B
δυστυχης	unlucky	5 A-B
εισ - φερ - **ω**	**I** bring in, **I** carry in	5 A-B
εν - ειμι	**I** am in	5 A-B
ἡδυς	sweet, pleasant	5 A-B
ὁ **ἱ**ππος	horse	5 A-B
κακα ποιε - **ω** κακως	**I** treat badly, **I** do harm to	5 A-B
κολαζ - **ω**	**I** punish	5 A-B

ὁ νεανιας 5 A-B	young man
νε - **ος** - **α** - **ον** 5 A-B	young
ὁ οικετης 5 A-B	house- slave
ὁλ - **ος** - **η** - **ον** 5 A-B	whole of
ουδεπ ω / ουπ ω 5 A-B	not yet
οφειλ - **ω** 5 A-B	**I** owe
ὁ πατηρ 5 A-B	father
παυ - **ω** 5 A-B	**I** stop
πειθ - **ομαι** 5 A-B	**I** trust, **I** obey, **I** believe

σχεδον	5 A-B	near, nearly, almost
τοτε	5 A-B	then
ὁ υἱος	5 A-B	son
φης	5 A-B	you say (singular)
τα χρεα	5 A-B	debts
τα χρηματα	5 A-B	money
χρηστ **- ος** **- η** **- ον**	5 A-B	good, fine, serviceable

Vocabulary 5 C-D

22 words

'Reading Greek'

αδικ - **ος** - **ον**	5 C-D	unjust
ἡ αιτια	5 C-D	reason, cause, responsibility
αυριον	5 C-D	tomorrow
δεχ - **ομαι**	5 C-D	**I** receive
διανοε - **ομαι**	5 C-D	**I** intend, **I** plan
ἡ διανοια	5 C-D	intention, plan
διδασκ - **ω**	5 C-D	**I** teach
δικαι - **ος** - **α** - **ον**	5 C- D	just

Greek	Ref.	English
εισ - ερχ - **ομαι**	5 C-D	I enter
ενδον	5 C-D	inside
και δη και	5 C-D	moreover
κοπ τ - **ω**	5 C-D	I knock (on), I cut
ὁ μαθητης	5 C-D	student
ὁ νους	5 C-D	mind, sense
ουδεποτε	5 C-D	never
ουτε....ουτε	5 C-D	neither....nor
πειθ - **ω**	5 C-D	I persuade

ὁ Ποσειδων

Poseidon

(god of sea)

5 C-D

πως

somehow

5 C-D

ὁ σοφιστης

sophist,
thinker

5 C-D

σοφ - **ος**
- **η**
- **ον**

5 C-
D

wise,
clever

φιλε - **ω**

I love,
I kiss,
I am used to

5 C-D

Vocabulary 6 A-D

55 words

'Reading Greek'

αγροικ **- ος** **- ον**	6 A-D	from the country, rustic, boorish
αδυνατ **- ος** **- ον**	6 A-D	impossible
αι Αθηναι	6 A-D	Athens
αμαθης	6 A-D	ignorant
απερχ **- ομαι**	6 A-D	**I** depart, **I** go away
αρα	6 A-D	then, in that case (inferring)
βαλλ' εις κορακας	6 A-D	go to hell !
βιαζ **- ομαι**	6 A-D	**I** use force

ὁ γερων	6 A-D	old man
ἡ γνωμη	6 A-D	mind, purpose, judgement, plan
δακν **- ω**	6 A-D	**I** bite, **I** worry
δεξι **- ος** **- α** **- ον**	6 A-D	right, clever
ἡ δεξια	6 A-D	right hand
ὁ δημος	6 A-D	deme, people
δητα	6 A-D	then
δρα **- ω**	6 A-D	**I** do, **I** act
ει	6 A-D	if

Greek	Ref.	English
ειτα	6 A-D	then, next
εκβαλλ - **ω**	6 A-D	I throw out, I divorce, I break open
εμαυτον	6 A-D	myself
εν νω εχ - **ω**	6 A-D	I intend, I have in mind
εξευρισκ - **ω**	6 A-D	I find out
ἑτερ - **ος** - **α** - **ον**	6 A-D	one (or the other) of two
ὁ **ἡ**λιος	6 A-D	sun
ἡττων **ἡ**ττον	6 A-D	lesser, weaker
θαυμαζ - **ω**	6 A-D	I wonder at, I am amazed at, I wonder

Greek	Ref.	English
καιπερ	6 A-D	although (+part)
ἡ κεφαλη	6 A-D	head
κλεπ τ - **ω**	6 A-D	I steal
κρειττων κρειττον	6 A-D	stronger, greater
λυ - **ω**	6 A-D	I release
ὁποσ - **ος** - **η** - **ον**	6 A-D	how much, how many
ὁ π ου	6 A-D	where
ὁτε	6 A-D	when (ὁ…)
ὁ ουρανος	6 A-D	sky, heavens

οὑτος	6 A-D	hey there ! hey you !
πανυ	6 A-D	very (much), at all
π ηδα - **ω**	6 A-D	**I** leap, **I** jump
πορρω	6 A-D	I am far, I am far off
ποτερ - **ος** - **α** - **ον**	6 A-D	which (of two) ?
ὁ πους	6 A-D	foot
πρωτον	6 A-D	first, at first
πρωτ - **ος** - **η** - **ον**	6 A-D	first
ῥαδι - **ος** - **α** - **ον**	6 A-D	easy

Greek	Ref.	English
ῥαδιως	6 A-D	easily
ἡ σεληνη	6 A-D	moon
σ - **ος** - **η** - **ον**	6 A-D	your(s) (when ‘you‘ is one person)
ὁ Σωκρατης	6 A-D	Socrates
τημερον	6 A-D	today
τ**ί** ;	6 A-D	why ?
τιθημι	6 A-D	**I** put, **I** place
ἡ φροντις	6 A-D	thought, care, concern
χρησιμ - **ος** - **η** - **ον**	6 A-D	useful, profitable

το χωριον 6 A-D	place, space, region
ὡς 6 A-D	as

Vocabulary 7 A-C

29 words

'Reading Greek'

ἡ αληθεια	truth	7 A-C
αναγκη εστι	it is obligatory (for X)to …	7 A-C
ἡ αναγκη	necessity	7 A-C
αποφαιν - **ω**	**I** reveal, **I** show	7 A-C
βουλ - **ομαι**	**I** wish, **I** want	7 A-C
γαρ δη	really, I assure you	7 A-C
δει	it is necessary (for X) to ….	7 A-C
διαβαλλ - **ω**	**I** slander	7 A-C

ἡ διαβολη 7 A-C	slander
δοκε - **ω** 7 A-C	I seem (to myself), I consider myself to ..
ἡ δοξα 7 A-C	reputation, opinion
ἑαυτ - **ον** - **ην** - **ο** 7 A-C	himself, herself, itself
ειδ - **ως** - **υια** - **ος** 7 A-C	knowing
ειμι 7 A- C	I shall go
εντευθεν 7 A-C	from then, from there
εξεταζ - **ω** 7 A-C	I question closely

εὑρισκ - **ω**	7 A-C	**I** find, **I** come upon
η	7 A-C	than
ισως	7 A-C	perhaps
λογιζ - **ομαι**	7 A-C	**I** reckon , **I** calculate, **I** consider
νοε - **ω**	7 A-C	**I** think, **I** notice, **I** mean, **I** intend
οιμαι	7 A-C	I think
παρειμι	7 A-C	I am present, I am at hand
πειρα - **ομαι**	7 A-C	**I** try, **I** test
ὁ ποιητης	7 A-C	poet

Greek	English	Ref.
πολλακις	often	7 A-C
ποτε	once, ever	7 A-C
ἡ σοφια	wisdom	7 A-C
ὡς	that	7 A-C

Vocabulary 7 D-F

20 words

'Reading Greek'

ανδρ - **εις** - **α** - **ον**	7 D-F	brave, manly
αποκριν - **ομαι**	7 D-F	I answer
ἡ αρετη	7 D-F	virtue, excellence
γελα - **ω**	7 D-F	I laugh
δηπου	7 D-F	of course, surely
ὁ διδασκαλος	7 D-F	teacher
εκδεχ - **ομαι**	7 D-F	I receive in turn
εμ πι π τ - **ω**	7 D-F	I fall into , I fall on

επαινε - **ω** 7 D-F	**I** praise
ευθυς 7 D-F	at once, straightaway
ἡδ - **ομαι** 7 D-F	**I** enjoy, **I** am pleased
ην δ'εγω 7 D-F	**I** said
η δ'ος 7 D-F	he said
ὁμολογε - **ω** 7 D-F	**I** agree
ουκουν 7 D-F	therefore
ουκουν 7 D-F	not ......therefore
ὁ νεανισκος 7 D-F	young man

προτρεπ - **ω** 7 D-F	**I** urge on, **I** impel
φημι 7 D-F	I say
ἡ φιλοσοφια 7 D-F	philosophy

Vocabulary 7 G-H

29 words

'Reading Greek'

αγ - **ω**	7 G-H	I lead, I bring
αναιρε - **ω**	7 G-H	I pick up
απο - βαιν - **ω**	7 G-H	I leave, I depart
αυτ - **ος** / - **η** / - **ο**	7 G-H	self
διαβαιν - **ω**	7 G-H	I cross
δυναμαι	7 G-H	I am able
δυο	7 G-H	two
αὑτ - **ον** / - **ην** / - **ο**	7 G-H	himself, herself, itself

ἑαυτ - **ους** - **ας** - **α**	7 G-H	themselves (e..)
α**ὑ**τ - **ους** - **ας** - **α**	7 G-H	themselves (a..)
επανερχ - **ομαι**	7 G-H	I return
ἑπ - **ομαι**	7 G-H	I follow
ἡμας αυτους αυτας	7 G-H	ourselves
κατα- λαμβαν - **ω**	7 G-H	I come across, I overtake
το κτημα	7 G-H	possession, acquisition
ἡ μαχη	7 G-H	fight, battle

μεντοι

7 G-H

however,
but

μετα	7 G-H	after
νομιζ - **ω**	7 G-H	**I** think, **I** acknowledge
ὁ αυτος	7 G-H	the same
οικε - **ω**	7 G-H	**I** dwell (in), **I** live
παλιν	7 G-H	back, again
ὁ ποταμος	7 G-H	river
το σημειον	7 G-H	sign, signal
ὑμας αυτους αυτας	7 G-H	yourselves
ὑμετερ - **ος** - **α** - **ον**	7 G-H	your (s) (pl)

φυλαττ - **ω**	7 G-H	**I** guard
φωνε - **ω**	7 G-H	**I** speak, **I** utter
ἡ φωνη	7 G-H	voice, language, speech

Vocabulary 8 A - C

56 words

'Reading Greek'

ἡ αγορα	8 A-C	market - place, agora
αδικε - **ω**	8 A-C	I am unjust, I commit a crime, I do wrong
αδ - **ω** / αειδ - **ω**	8 A-C	I sing
ανιστ - **αμαι**	8 A-C	I get up I emigrate
αξι - **ος** - **α** - **ον**	8 A-C	worth, worthy of
απολε - **ω**	8 A-C	I shall kill, I shall destroy
βελτιστ - **ος** - **η** - **ον**	8 A-C	best
βελτιων βελτιον	8 A-C	better

Greek	Ref.	English
δια	8 A-C	through
το δικαςτηριον	8 A-C	law-court
ὁ δικαστης	8 A-C	juror, dikast
ἡ ειρηνη	8 A-C	peace
ειρηνην αγ **- ω**	8 A-C	**I** live in peace, **I** am at peace
εκεισε	8 A-C	(to) there
ἡ εκκλησια	8 A-C	assembly, ekklesia
εναντιον	8 A-C	opposite, in front of
εν τουτω	8 A-C	meanwhile

Greek	Ref.	English
επει	8 A-C	since, when
επ ι	8 A-C	on, in the time of
ἑτοιμ - **ος** - **η** - **ον**	8 A-C	ready to (+inf.)
ευ - δαιμ - **ων** ευ - δαιμ - **ον**	8 A-C	happy, rich, blessed by the gods
ὁ **ἡ**γεμων	8 A-C	leader
ἡγε - **ομαι**	8 A-C	**I** think, **I** consider, **I** lead
ἡ **ἡ**δονη	8 A-C	pleasure
ὁ **Ἡ**ρακλης	8 A-C	Herakles
καθορα - **ω**	8 A-C	**I** see, **I** look down on

λαμβαν - **ομαι**	8 A-C	I take hold of
μετα	8 A-C	with
μεγιστ - **ος** - **η** - **ον**	8 A-C	biggest, greatest
μειζ - **ων** μειζ - **ον**	8 A-C	greater
μον - **ος** - **η** - **ον**	8 AC	alone
μων ;	8 A-C	surely not ?
νυν	8 A-C	so, then
οικτιρ - **ω**	8 A-C	I pity
ὁ μεν.......**ὁ** δε	8 A-C	one.....another

Greek	Ref.	English
το παθος	8 A-C	experience, suffering
πανταχου	8 A-C	everywhere
πεμπ - **ω**	8 A-C	I send
περι	8 A-C	about
πλε - **ως** - **α** - **ων**	8 A- C	full of
ποιε - **ομαι**	8 A-C	I make
ὁ πολιτης	8 A-C	citizen
προσ - τρεχ - **ω**	8 A-C	I run towards
ὁ ῥητωρ	8 A-C	orator, speaker, politician

ὁ σιτος (pl. τα σιτα)	8 A-C	food
αι σ πονδαι	8 A-C	treaty, truce
ὁ συγγενης	8 A-C	relation
ταν	8 A-C	my dear chap
ὑπερ	8 A-C	for, on behalf of
ὑπο	8 A-C	by, at the hands of
ὁ φιλοσοφος	8 A-C	philosopher
χαιρε	8 A-C	hello ! farewell !
χαλεπ **- ος - η - ον**	8 A-C	difficult, hard

ἡ χειρ 8 A-C	hand
χειρ **- ων** **- ον** 8 A-C	worse
ὁ χρονος 8 A-C	time

Vocabulary 9 A-E

38 words

'Reading Greek'

αμειν **- ων**
- ον

better

9 A-E

ὁ αναξ

prince,
lord,
king

9 A-E

ανα - πειθ **- ω**

I persuade over to my side

9 A-E

ανω

up,
above

9 A-E

απο - τρεχ **- ω**

I run away

9 A-E

βαρεως φερ **- ω**

I take badly,
I find hard to bear

9 A-E

δικαζ **- ω**

I am a juror,
I make a judgement

9 A-E

δοκει

it seems a good idea to X to ....
X decides to ....

9 A-E

το δραμα	9 A-E	play, drama
εγκλει **- ω**	9 A-E	I shut in, I lock in
εκ - φευγ **- ω**	9 A-E	I escape
ενταυθα	9 A-E	here , at this point
εντυγχαν **- ω**	9 A-E	I meet with
εξ - αγ **- ω**	9 A-E	I lead out, I bring out
εξ- ερχ **- ομαι**	9 A-E	I go out, I come out
ἡ ἡμερα	9 A-E	day
ὁ ἡμιονος	9 A-E	mule

ἡσυχ - **ος** - **ον**	9 A-E	quiet, peaceful
ὁ θεατης	9 A-E	spectator, member of audience
καθιζ - **ομαι**	9 A-E	I sit down
καθιζ - **ω**	9 A-E	I sit down
μελ - **ας** - **αινα** - **αν**	9 A-E	black
μηκετι	9 A-E	no longer
μιαρ - **ος** - **α** - **ον**	9 A-E	foul, polluted
ὁμοι - **ος** - **α** - **ον**	9 A-E	like, similar to
το ονομα	9 A-E	name

Greek	Ref.	English
παρεχ - **ω**	9 A-E	**I** give to, **I** provide
πλησιον	9 A-E	nearby, near
πονηρ - **ος** - **α** - **ον**	9 A-E	wicked, wretched
πραγματα παρεχ - **ω**	9 A-E	**I** cause trouble
προς	9 A-E	near, in addition to
πωλε - **ω**	9 A-E	**I** sell
σ τεν - **ω**	9 A-E	**I** groan
συν	9 A-E	with (the help of)
ταλ - **ας** - **αινα** - **αν**	9 A-E	wretched, unhappy

τοι - **ουτος** - **αυτη** - **ουτο(ν)** 9 A- E	of this kind, of such a kind
φερε 9 A-E	come !
χρα - **ομαι** 9 A-E	**I** use, **I** employ

Vocabulary 9 F- G

17 words

'Reading Greek'

αναμεν - **ω**	I wait, I hold on
9 F- G	
αρχ - **ομαι**	I begin to....
9 F- G	
αταρ	but
9 F- G	
εα - **ω**	I allow
9 F- G	
εκ - τρεχ - **ω**	I run out
9 F- G	
εκ - φερ - **ω**	I carry out
9 F- G	
ενεκα	because, for the sake of
9 F- G	
ενθαδε	here
9 F- G	

εξεστι	it is possible for X to …)
9 F- G	
εσθι - **ω**	**I** eat
9 F- G	
ὁμως	nevertheless, however
9 F- G	
ὁ τι ;	what ?
9 F- G	
πα - **ς** **- σα** **- ν**	all, every
9 F- G	
ὁ πας	the whole of
9 F- G	
πλην	except
9 F- G	
το πυρ	fire
9 F- G	
χρη	it is necessary/ right for X to ….
9 F- G	

Vocabulary 9 H - J

36 words

'Reading Greek'

αἱρε - **ω**	9 H - J	I take, I capture, I convict
αιτε - **ω**	9 H - J	I ask (for)
αμφοτερ - **οι** - **αι** - **α**	9 H - J	both
απολογε - **ομαι**	9 H - J	I defend myself I make a speech in my own defense
ἡ απολογια	9 H - J	speech in one's own defense
απολυ - **ω**	9 H - J	I acquit, I release
αυ	9 H - J	again, moreover
ἡ γραφη	9 H - J	indictment, charge, case

γραφ - **ομαι**	I indict , I charge	9 H - J
γραφην γραφ - **ομαι**	I indict X on a charge of Y	9 H - J
εθελ - **ω**	I wish, I want (to)	9 H - J
ελπ ιζ - **ω**	I hope, I expect	9 H - J
εξ - απ ατα - **ω**	I deceive, I trick	9 H - J
επ ιστ - **αμαι**	I know how to, I understand	9 H - J
ὁ θανατος	death	9 H - J
κατα - δικαζ - **ω**	I condemn, I convict X on a charge of Y	9 H - J
κατηγορε - **ω**	I prosecute X on a charge of Y	9 H - J

speech for the prosecution

9 H - J

Greek	Ref.	English
ὁ κλεπ της	9 H - J	thief
ὁ κυων	9 H - J	dog
ὁ μαρτυς	9 H - J	witness
μελλ - **ω**	9 H - J	**I** am about to … **I** intend, **I** hesitate
το μερος	9 H - J	share, part
ὁ δε **ἡ** δε **το** δε	9 H - J	this here
ὁτι	9 H - J	because
το παιδιον	9 H - J	child, young slave
παρα (+gen.)	9 H - J	from

πολυ 9 H - J	much
προς 9 H - J	in the name of, under the protection of
συγγνωμην εχ **- ω** 9 H - J	**I** forgive, **I** pardon
τυγχαν **- ω** 9 H - J	**I** hit, **I** chance on, **I** happen on, **I** am subject to
ὑπ ισ χνε **- ομαι** 9 H - J	**I** promise to
ὑσ τερ **- ος** **- α** **- ον** 9 H - J	later, last (of two)
ὑσ τερον 9 H - J	later, further
ὑφαιρε **- ομαι** 9 H - J	**I** steal, **I** take for myself by stealth
ἡ ψηφος 9 H - J	vote, voting-pebble

Printed in Great Britain
by Amazon